W9-AUX-981

TRAINS

JAMES GIBB

METRO BOOKS
NEW YORK

© 2010 by TAJ Books International LLP

This 2010 edition published by Metro Books,
by arrangement with TAJ Books International LLP.

All rights reserved. No part of this publication may be reproduced,
stored in a retrieval system, or transmitted, in any form or by any means,
electronic, mechanical, photocopying, recording, or otherwise,
without prior written permission from the publisher.

Metro Books
122 Fifth Avenue
New York, NY 10011

ISBN 10: 1-4351-2069-8
ISBN 13: 978-1-4351-2069-3

Printed and bound in China

1 3 5 7 9 10 8 6 4 2

Contents

Introduction

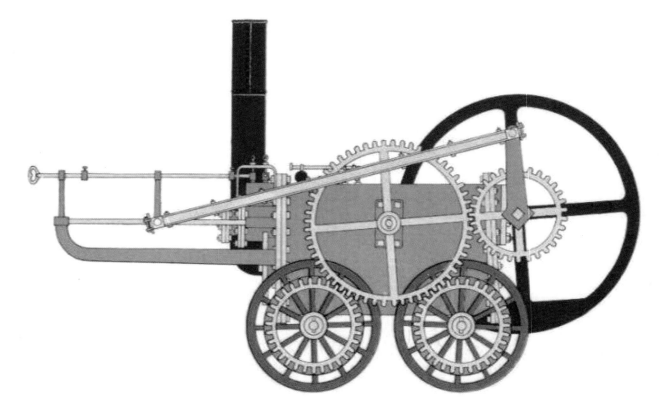

Richard Trevithick's unnamed locomotive made its first journey on February 21, 1804.

Railways changed the face of the world. They revolutionized the bulk transit of goods and people allowing industry to blossom by bringing raw materials and workers where they were needed. Rail travel also revolutionized concepts of personal mobility, allowing the individual the chance of traveling a greater distance faster than before. Within a hundred years of its invention, rail travel was possible on nearly a million miles of track worldwide, from the London underground commuter network to the massive Trans-Siberian Railway that crossed the frozen wastes of Asiatic Russia.

Crude railways—horse-drawn wagons with wooden wheels and rails—had been used in English and European mines during the seventeenth century. Between 1797 and 1813, Richard Trevithick and other early inventors adapted primitive steam locomotives to the mine railway. In 1825, George Stephenson completed and equipped the 20-mile-long Stockton and Darlington Railway, setting a precedent as the first public railway using steam locomotives, attracting great interest in Britain, America, and ultimately around the world. The speed of development of steam traction and railways was remarkable. Established first in Britain as power for light tram railways. "Railway Mania" had gripped the United States in the mid- and late nineteenth century. It was here that railways enjoyed their most dramatic growth, characterized by the story of the incorporation of the Baltimore & Ohio Railroad (B&O). Philip Evan Thomas (the "father of U.S. railways") and George Brown were instrumental in establishing the B&O to compete with canals, particular New York's famous Erie Canal for traffic to and from the interior of the United States. After dispatching engineers to study the British steam railways, Thomas and Brown's committee proposed a railway that was chartered in March 1827. Three years later, in May 1830, a short section of B&O was opened making it first public railway in the United States. Similar schemes were underway in, New England, New York, Pennsylvania, and South Carolina. Within a decade more than 3,000 miles of railroad were in operation in the eastern states—40 percent more than

Robert Stephenson's Rocket. The first "modern" locomotive.

A replica of Stephenson's Planet, first built in 1830.

Introduction

The footplate and controls of a steam locomotive with the fire door open. Proper start up of locomotive may take up from an hour to eight hours depending on outside temperature and size and condition of the locomotive.

the total railroad mileage of Europe. By the eve of the Civil War the network in the United States was more than 30,000 miles long, and the railroads of the western lines had nearly caught up with the ever-moving western frontier. The speed and hauling capacity of railroads was undeniable. By 1860 the efficiency of railway technology had clearly shown superiority over older established modes of transport, including turnpikes, canals, and steamboats. Following the Civil War several lines were extended across the continent to reach the Pacific coast. The first, the so-called "transcon," was built by Union Pacific and Central Pacific Railroads, joining famously at Promontory, Utah on May 10, 1869.

As industrial development reached Asia, Africa, South America, and Australia, so railways developed on those continents as the dominant form of transport. By the early decades of the twentieth century, nearly 900,000 miles of railroad had been built in the world, with some mileage in nearly every nation. In North America the route mileage was enormous and rapidly built: by 1890 the U.S. rail network had reached 163,000 route miles; at its zenith in 1916 it had reached 254,000 route miles. In Canada, railroad service began in 1836, and by 1880 its network had expanded to about 6,960 miles. The Canadian Pacific Railway was completed across the Rockies to the Pacific by 1885.

Even as railways expanded around the globe, signs of a decline in steam traction were apparent in the major industrialized nations after World War I. Early in the century the monopoly that had been held by steam railroads was challenged by a number of new modes of transport: electric tram and lightly built interurban electric lines; well-paved public-built roads and highways led to first thousands and later millions of private automobiles, intercity buses, and ever larger and larger

The roundhouse was quickly developed into the best way of housing and servicing locomotives. The first roundhouse was built in 1839 at England; a famous example in the United States is today's B&O Railroad Museum in Baltimore, Maryland. This restored roundhouse is said to be the world's largest 22-sided building. Pictured is Kolomyia depot in the Ukraine.

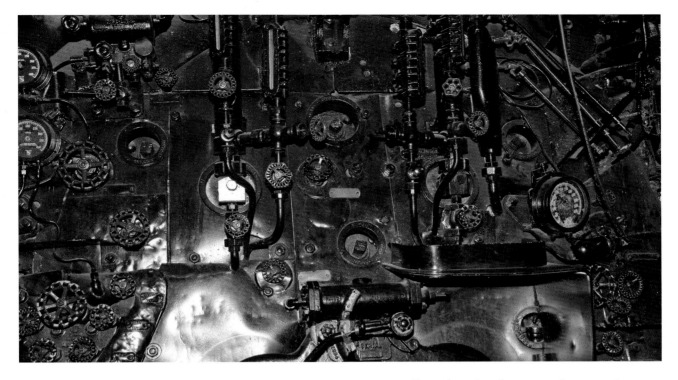

trucks; airplanes carrying mail, passengers, and high-priority freight; and a growing network of pipelines. As a result of modal competition, and fundamental changes in public policy and a rapid growth in wages railways in the United States and Europe went into slow decline after World War I, ultimately substantial losses in route mileage, employment, and market share.

The heavy wartime traffic saturated railways in the 1940s, leading to temporary recovery of traffic lost over the previous decades, and helped companies recover from the hard times of the Depression of the 1930s. However after the War, further public policy changes along with increased investment in highway and airline industries precluded a large scale railway renaissance. Despite short term profits in the railway industry in America, and technical advances—diesel-electric locomotives and automatic centralized signalling systems offered much greater efficiency through much improved worker productivity—nevertheless, by the mid-1970s, railways in Europe and the U.S. suffered badly as other modes continued to grow. By 1990 in Britain railway route mileage was 10,250 miles compared with 17,000 in 1900. The worldwide total of nearly one million miles of track had declined to about

More complicated engines have complex controls and valves.

800,000 miles, divided roughly as follows: Europe, 35 percent; North America, 30 percent; Asia, 17 percent; South America, 7.5 percent; Africa, 6.8 percent; and Australasia, 3.7 percent. But as a new millennium dawned, around the world governments realized the importance of maintaining rail—as a more sustainable and "green" method of transport.

Locomotive development

Lightly built tram railways had been used for centuries—mainly in mines—employing gravity or animal power to move carts along wooden tracks or stone plateways. But it was at the end of the eighteenth century and the beginning of the nineteenth that steam engines were developed to the point of haulage. William Murdoch, a Scottish inventor, built a prototype steam road locomotive in 1784. The first-known working model of a steam rail locomotive was designed and constructed by John Fitch in the United States in 1794. Then in 1804 British inventor Richard Trevithick built the first full scale working railway steam locomotive.

Introduction

On February 21, 1804, the world's first steam powered railway journey took place as Trevithick's *Pen-y-Darran* engine, a crudely built one-cylinder powered flywheel steam locomotive hauled a train along the Penydarren ironworks tramway, near Merthyr Tydfil in Wales. Further steam locomotive development took place in Wylam on Tyne in England under the auspices of mineowner Christopher Blackett. Wylam was the birthplace of George Stephenson (the so-called "father of railways"), who would go on to build the world's first public railway. The first locomotive superintendent of that railway—the Stockton & Darlington—Timothy Hackworth, worked t here too, as did another famous name in steam railway development, William Hedley, who built *Puffing Billy* and *Wylam Dilly*, two of the oldest surviving steam locomotives in the world. In 1812 Matthew Murray built a rack locomotive for the world's oldest continuously worked railway—the Middleton Railway. These early efforts culminated in 1829 with the Rainhill Trials and the opening of the Liverpool and Manchester Railway a year later, making exclusive use of steam power for both passenger and freight trains.

In the U.S. there was early interest in locomotives. In New Jersey, early railway promoter John Stevens demonstrated a "steam wagon" on his Hoboken estate in 1825. More significantly, in 1827 Delaware & Hudson, a coal moving canal company, started work on a 17-mile tramway to tap Anthracite mines in eastern Pennsylvania and imported four locomotives from Britain in 1828-1829. On one, the *Stourbridge Lion*, was tested in service in August 1829. Although deemed to heavy for work on the line, it stirred national interest in locomotives.

Equally important, B&O developed an interest in steam locomotives. In August 1830, New York glue-maker and budding industrialist, Peter Cooper demonstrated the first American designed and built locomotive to B&O. This engine was famously recalled as the *Tom Thumb*. Other railways quickly followed the B&O—such as the South Carolina Railroad whose inaugural train ran on December 25, 1830, hauled by the *Best Friend of Charleston*. Many of the earliest locomotives for American railroads were imported from England, among these were several named *John Bull*. Although some American lines continued to import British-built engines during the 1830s, a domestic locomotive manufacturing industry was quickly established. Some of the earliest American engines, such as *Tom Thumb* and its successors, were derived from marine practice and established a line of home-grown engineering, however most were derived from British practice and related to Robert Stephenson's precedent setting *Rocket* of 1829.

The steam locomotive would grow in size and power until such massive powerful as the Union Pacific's "Big Boys"—huge articulated engines 132 feet 9 3/8 inches in length, capable of producing more than 7,000hp.

Steam locomotives dominated railway traction from the start of the nineteenth century until the middle of the twentieth. They were steadily improved over 150 years of development but from the end of the nineteenth century electric traction made inroads into this hegemony. Benefiting from being smokeless—in particular for underground and urban use—electric traction quickly took over from steam in countries such as Switzerland, where its better traction on slopes and cleanliness in tunnels made it much more efficient than

Steam power did not only drive the locos—it helped build and maintain them. Here blacksmiths use a small steam drop hammer at the Atchison, Topeka and Santa Fe Railway shops in Topeka, Kansas, 1943.

steam, and in urban areas such as New York or southeast England.

Electric units are cleaner, because electric motors do not pollute the environment, and their power is supplied centrally from a large generating plant, which produces its power more efficiently and cleanly than individual diesel locomotives do. Electric locomotives are relatively simple to construct, have a low maintenance cost, and have a longer economic life than diesel units. The major disadvantages of electrified service are the high upfront costs needed to build the infrastructure: the catenary needed to carry overhead wire, power substations, and other necessary equipment. On top of this, electric locomotives lack the flexibility of diesel power, because they can operate only where a third rail or overhead wires are in place. Because of this, electric operation was initially profitable only in areas of large population or dense traffic. Such conditions prevail in most countries in Europe—particularly the commuter lines around London and Southeast England—as well as in Japan, Russia and in a few major U.S. cities: New York, Philadelphia, and Chicago. However, such is its versatility that most of the major mainlines in continental Europe from Iberia to the Urals and from beyond the Arctic Circle to the boot of Italy are now electrified. The Russian mainline network is largely electrified, including the Trans-Siberian. Some electrified services are in place in South America, Australia, and in Africa.

From the middle of the twentieth century diesel traction was developed to become the dominant form of locomotive power in most parts of the world. Although the original engine was invented in the 1890s by Rudolf Diesel, a French-born German mechanical engineer, it wasn't until the 1920s and 1930s, when significant metallurgical advances and development of practical high-pressure fuel injection systems that the diesel engine was developed into a reliable compact high-output locomotive power plant

The superior thermal efficiency of the diesel engine, the ability to work engines in multiple, combined with much lower maintenance costs, and higher locomotive availability, and relatively low fuel costs offset the diesel's higher per unit cost making it the preferred form of motive power.

Traditional steam locomotives required extensive daily attention to their firebox and boiler, while diesels can run thousands of miles with only incidental maintenance. Using an electric transmission a diesel locomotive transmits power to the wheels more smoothly, avoiding damaging forces caused steam-engine's unbalanced reciprocating motion that damaged track. There are many other advantages as well: as with electric locomotives, a diesel-electric can use its motors as brakes on downgrades, which reduces wear on train brakes and allows for operation of much heavier trains. Diesels offer greater flexibility, require far less specialization, and enabling railways to use just a few types in a great variety of service.

United States of America

All over the western world the Industrial Revolution led to the proliferation of the steam locomotive and the United States proved one of the greatest producers of locomotives. Carrying people and freight behind it, the iron horse conquered the vast intercontinental distances of North America leaving the canal, stagecoach, and wagon irrelevant with its capacity for pulling large loads for long distances.

While several short industrial tramway were built in American in the early years of the nineteenth century, in 1826 Gridley Bryant's Granite Railway in Massachusetts was the first commercial railroad chartered and built in the United States. Although not initially a steam railroad, this pioneer enterprise attracted great attention, and even warranted a private tour of the President of the United States. Once the railroad took root, it grew rapidly. When, on May 10, 1869, the transcontinental railroad was completed at Promontory, Utah, it was symbol of man's progress and

freight by rail; but, by 2000, the share of U.S. rail freight was 38 percent while in Europe only 8 percent of freight traveled by rail. In 1997, while U.S. trains moved 2,165 billion ton-kilometers of freight, the European Union moved only 238 billion ton-kilometers of freight.

As steam locomotives were replaced by other modes, people began to realize that there was more to the steam railway than just an inefficient old transport system: the great locomotives were awesome, powerful behemoths that came alive when they ran, belching smoke and steam and sparks. People began to preserve these mechanical marvels and buy up stretches of line to run them on. Pretty soon this preservation movement, which had started out as a labor of love, became a part of the tourist industry and now the wheel has turned full circle. Preserved locomotives and historic railways have generated great interest in modern times attracting tens of thousands of visitors annually.

Pennsylvania Railroad No. 4483 is the only surviving example of the company's 598 standard Class I1s 2-10-0 "Decapods" built for heavy freight service between 1916 and 1924. (Note the "s" in I1s, indicates superheating.)

Although America imported a significant number of British locomotives in their formative years of railway development, since the late 1830s, most of the locomotives built for American railways have been domestically designed and produced. The desire to develop American industry was key to the early development of railways in New England, New York, and Pennsylvania. As railways took hold, several domestic manufacturers emerged to supply American railways with adequate motive power. The more cheaply constructed nature of American railway lines demanded locomotives with a more flexible wheelbase than those used on early British railways. As a result many of the early imports had derailed too frequently. This fundamental difference, combined with the large clearances afforded American railroads, led to an early divergence in locomotive design and application. While many railroads ordered specifically designed locomotives from either commercial manufacturers or company shops, on occasion old locomotives would be sold from one railroad to another.

United States of America

This Baldwin-built 2-6-2 "Prairie" was typical of locomotives designed for light branch-line freight service.

This old "one spot" is an unusual 2-4-0T type for timber service with a unusually large stack with spark arrestors.

Locomotives for timber service used a variety of elaborate spark arrestors to prevent forest fires. In 1891, Baldwin built Surrey, Sussex & Southampton No. 6. Today it survives dressed up as tourist locomotive.

The 4-6-4 Hudson was an advancement of the 4-6-2 Pacific type and largely used for fast passenger service. Santa Fe bought some of the finest Hudsons, beginning in 1926 with Baldwin-built No. 3450.

Santa Fe's Baldwin-built 2-10-4 Texas types had the greatest piston thrust of any American locomotive ever built. No. 5021 was from the final order, built to satisfy wartime traffic in 1944. Today it is preserved at the California State Railroad Museum in Sacramento.

Union Pacific 2-8-0 No. 1068 has been a popular attraction on Utah's Heber Valley Railroad. For operational clarification Union Pacific and Southern Pacific place train numbers, rather than locomotive numbers in the number boards, thus locomotive 1068 leads train No. 98.

Santa Fe's first Hudson, No. 3450, is one of the only a few preserved 4-6-4s in the United States. It serves as a static display at the Los Angeles County Fairplex in Pomona, California.

A rare 1940s color view of Santa Fe Railway's Argentine Yards near Kansas City.

Traditionally, the Santa Fe Railway was the only railroad under one management to connect Chicago with California. In the 1940s, a Santa Fe freight departs Chicago Corwith Yard.

These three views depict Pere Marquette 2-8-4 Berkshire No. 1225 in winter excursion work in Michigan. The 2-8-4 was developed by Lima in 1924-1925 for Boston & Albany and named for the Berkshire Hills of Massachusetts. The PM 2-8-4 represents a refinement of the original design with taller drive wheels for fast freight service.

Lima's semi-streamlined 4-8-4s were built for Southern Pacific passenger service in the late 1930s and early 1940s and are seen here dressed for the Daylight. The best of the class were SP's Gs-4s built in 1941. The original streamlined Daylight services operated between San Francisco and Los Angeles via the Coast Line. The commercial success of Daylight spawned a whole family of Daylight trains on SP's lines in California. Portland, Oregon based SP Gs-4 No. 4449 was preserved and restored to its 1941 livery in 1981.v

CB&Q (Chicago, Burlington and Quincy Railroad) 2-8-2 No. 4960 was rebuilt for heavy daily excursion service on Grand Canyon Railway.

Much to the horror of the traveling public, No. 4960 was retired from active service a few years ago in favor of lower cost diesel operation.

CB&Q 2-8-2 No. 4960 was typical of the Mikado type.

Roaring Camp & Big Trees No. 3 Dixiana is a two-truck geared "Shay" built for lumber service.

Built for timber service, McCloud River Railroad's Baldwin 2-8-2 was a popular excursion engine in its later life.

More than 1,500 steam locomotives have been preserved in the United States. Most are relatively small industrial engines.

United States of America

Shay-type Dixiana is a popular attraction at Felton, California's Roaring Camp & Big Trees.

Dixiana is Shay-type was built by Lima in 1912 for Tennessee's Alaculsy Lumber Company.

Roaring Camp & Big Trees No. 7 is another example of a geared Shay.

Spokane, Portland & Seattle No. 700 is a 4-8-4 Northern-type built by Baldwin in 1938.

This restored Prairie type makes for a static display in Washington State.

Mount Rainier Scenic Railroad No. 17 is an Alco-built 2-8-2T tank engine.

United States of America

Rio Grande class K-37 No. 499 was built as a standard gauge 2-8-0 but was later converted to a three-foot gauge 2-8-2 by the company shops.

Durango & Silverton's former Rio Grande 2-8-2 is ready for service at Durango, Colorado.

The Cumbres & Toltec Scenic Railroad operates 66 miles of former Rio Grande narrow gauge using the railroad's specially built 2-8-2 Mikados.

United States of America

Valley Railroad based at Essex, Connecticut uses hand-me-down Alco-built 2-8-2s in regular excursion service.

Valley Railroad 2-8-0 No. 97 often works on this old New Haven Railroad branch line revived in the 1970s a an excursion line.

Built for branch-line coal service, Chesapeake & Ohio 2-6-6-2 No. 1309 articulated is displayed at the B&O Museum in Baltimore.

United States of America

Three views of Nevada Northern Railway, locomotive 2-8-0 No. 93, seen at the East Ely Yards, NV., where it runs tourist excursions along the heritage "Ore Line" between Ely and Ruth, and Ely and McGill.

No. 93 approaching Steptoe Creek. The locomotive was built in 1909 at Alco Pittsburgh Works to work the Nevada Northern Railway ore route. In 1961 the engine was gifted to the White Pine Public Museum where it was restored to operating standards by volunteer enthusiasts.

Western Maryland Scenic uses a former Lake Superior & Ishpeming 2-8-0—No. 734—as its regular excursion engine on a segment of the old Western Maryland Railway.

Western Maryland Scenic No. 734 resembles one of the big 2-8-0 Consolidation types once used by the old Western Maryland Railway.

Preserved at the Cass Scenic Railroad, this three-truck geared Heisler type worked for West Virginia's Meadow Valley Lumber Company.

United States of America

Valley Railroad's star locomotive—No. 97—is an Alco-built 2-8-0 Consolidation from 1926.

Most of New York Central's late-era steam met the scrappers torch, an exception is class L3a Mohawk No. 3001 preserved at Elkhart, Indiana.

One of America's most famous passenger locomotives was Pennsylvania Railroad's class K4s Pacific.

United States of America

A pair of Chicago & North Western locomotives drill freight cars near Chicago in the 1940s.

Wartime work: the original 1940s caption identifies Mrs. Viola Sievers working as one of the wipers at the Clinton, Iowa roundhouse of the Chicago and North Western Railway. She is giving a giant C&NWRR "H" class locomotive a live steam bath in April 1943.

The C&NWRR locomotive shops in Chicago taken by photographer Jack Delano in December 1942.

Canada

This 1910-built 2-6-0 was constructed by Canadian Locomotive Company for Canada's Grand Trunk Railway.

Canada's railway history starts in the eighteenth century when horse-drawn wagons were used to haul stone at Louisbourg fortress. An incline railway, powered by a steam engine, was used in the 1820s during the building of the citadel at Quebec, and another railway was used from Hog's Back quarry, Ottawa, during the building of the Rideau Canal. The first proper railway, the Champlain and St. Lawrence Railroad, opened on July 21, 1836—a seasonal portage railway connecting river traffic from La Prairie on the St. Lawrence to St. Johns on the Richelieu River. Soon after it was followed the Albion Mines Railway in Stellarton, Nova Scotia which opened on September 19, 1839. This was built to carry coal from the mines to the loading pier at Dunbar Point. Another short line—the Montreal and Lachine Railroad, built to supplement water transportation—opened in 1847.

Two years later the Guarantee Act of 1849, which guaranteed interest on half the bonds of a railway longer than 75 miles, led to rapid expansion of Canadian railways such as the Great Western Railway. This was completed from Niagara Falls to Windsor in January 1854, and the largest rail project of the period—the Grand Trunk Railway— linked Montreal to Sarnia finished in 1860.

The railways helped the population expand into new territories, pushed the agricultural and timber frontiers westward and northward, and sustained emerging urban centers. Indeed, Canadian confederation in 1867 would promote the second phase of railway building in Canada. "Bonds of steel as well as of sentiment were needed to hold the new Confederation together. Without railways there would be and could be no Canada." The Intercolonial Railway was written into the Constitution Act—the union would push for the construction of railroads linking British North America. The Maritimes joined because of promises to build the Intercolonial Railway, and British Columbia because of a promise to build a transcontinental railroad—an enormous expenditure for a nation of only 3.5 million people. The transcontinental railway was completed by November 7, 1885, and the first passenger train left Montreal in June 1886, arriving in Port Moody, British Columbia, on July 4. Then the longest railway in the world, it was a marvelous feat of engineering. It was followed by the National Transcontinental Railway—

constructed between 1903 and 1912—a line from Moncton to Winnipeg, passing through the vast and uninhabited hinterland of the Canadian Shield. The third transcontinental route—the Canadian Northern Railway from Quebec to Vancouver via Ottawa, Winnipeg, and Edmonton—was incorporated in 1899 and finshed twenty years later.

The outbreak of the First World War in 1914 saw major railways nationalized and in 1923—as in the United Kingdom—they were merged into the Canadian National Railways in 1923. As in the United States, this was the peak of the railways in Canada. The growth of personal auto availability and, especially after World War 2, passenger airlines saw railways superseded. In 1978 the government created VIA Rail which took over all national passenger service in the country. In November 1995 the government privatized CN.

Canadian railways made extensive use of American steam locomotives in the early years. In the 20th century, the CPR bought and built hundreds of Ten-Wheeler type 4-6-0s for passenger and freight service and similar quantities of 2-8-0s and 2-10-2s for freight. 2-10-2s were also used in passenger service on mountain routes. It also bought 4-6-2 Pacifics between 1906 and 1948. The CPR had its own manufacturing facilities in Montreal, initially the DeLorimer shops and then the massive Angus Shops that replaced them in 1904.

Probably the best-known Canadian steam locomotives were the 4-6-4 Hudsons—or "Twenty Eight Hundreds (2800s)"—were hugely capable large locomotives first built in 1929. The semi-streamlined "H1" class Royal Hudsons were given that name because one—No. 2850 preserved in the Exporail exhibit hall of the Canadian Railway Museum in St. Constant (Delson) Quebec—hauled King George VI and Queen Elizabeth on the 1939 Royal Tour across Canada. Another of the class, No. 2860, saw use on excursions on the British Columbia Railway between 1974 and 1999.

The largest—and last—steam locomotives to run in Canada were 2-10-4 Selkirk locomotives, They received the first in 1929 and the last twenty years later.

Canadian National No. 7312 is a typical 0-6-0 switcher.

Canada

CPR H1b Hudson No. 2816 Empress leads an excursion in the Canadian Rockies.

Canadian Pacific Railway No. 2024 started out as a switcher for the U. S. Army. In 1967, it was donated to the Heritage Park in Calgary, Alberta, where it was renumbered.

No. 2816 Empress exits a tunnel in the Canadian Rockies.

Canada

Former Canadian National Railways 2-6-0 No. 89 works Pennsylvania's Strasburg Rail Road.

This locomotive is named for the old Edmonton, Yukon & Pacific Railroad, completed in 1902 and largely abandoned by the 1950s.

Pennsylvania Railroad M1b No. 6755 is displayed at the Railroad Museum of Pennsylvania.

Canada

Alaska's White Pass & Yukon three-foot gauge operates this 2-8-2 in excursion service out of Skagway. The WP&U is an American line in Alaska, although its northern end once reached the Yukon.

Canadian Pacific Railway N2b Consolidation 3716 was built by Alco affiliate Montreal Locomotive Works in 1912.

Seaboard Air Line No. 544 is a 2-10-0 Decapod on display at the North Carolina Transportation Museum in Spencer, North Carolina.

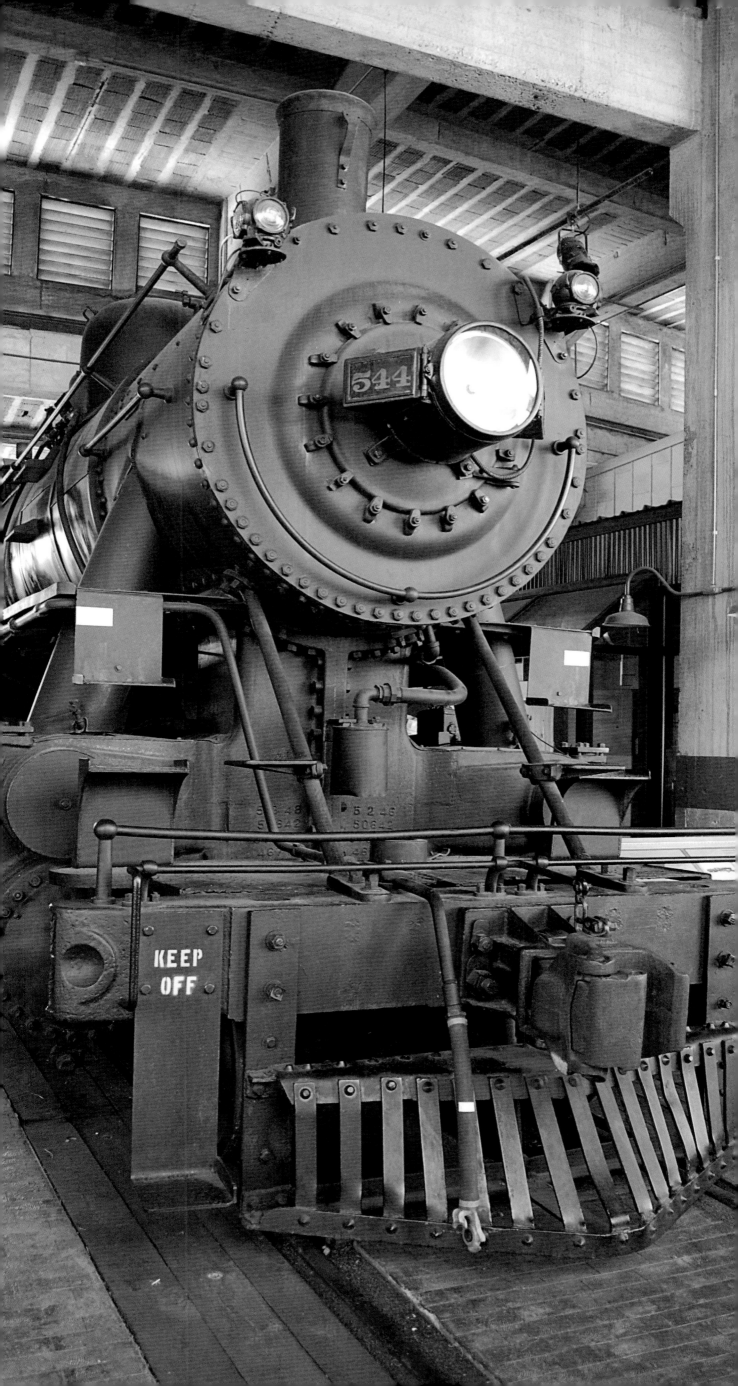

Great Britain

As has been discussed in the Introduction, the Industrial Revolution fired the growth of Britain's railways and forced the pace of early railway development. The Victorians embraced railways and the "Railway Mania" saw large numbers of companies incorporated, track mileage built, and wonderful structures erected—bridges, viaducts, tunnels, stations, and all the infrastructure needed to run a railway system. Railways were a force for change in Britain and everything from the imposition of standard time around the country, the growth of middle England's beer production, and the arrival of the seaside holiday were promoted by railways. The myriad speculative companies set up as the railways developed required engines and each produced or bought in its own locomotives, but as the economics of scale forced the companies to coalesce into larger entities, so the number of locomotive manufacturers reduced. By the late nineteenth century there were still over twenty mainline railway companies in the UK, all with distinctive traction needs, as well as a large number of industrial lines such as those that serviced the coal mines of the Welsh valleys. Britain developed many different types of locomotives but the size of the country meant that the huge long-distance engines required in the Americas or Russia did not develop in the UK.

The railways were nationalized during World War I and the benefits of central control were recognized. Three years after the war the 1921 Railway Act led to the "Grouping" of all the railway companies in Britain into the Big Four: the Great Western, Southern, London & North Eastern, and London Midland & Scottish railways. For twenty-five years these companies produced many of the locomotives beloved by enthusiasts today: the products of great mechanical engineers such as William Stanier on the LMS, Nigel Gresley on the LNER, Richard Maunsell and Oliver Bulleid on the Southern, and Collett and Hawksworth on the GWR.

British Railways "Black Five" 4-6-0 No. 45407 The Lancashire Fusilier was built in 1937. The "Black Fives"—LMS Class 5—were designed by William Stanier and 842 were built between 1934 and 1951.

World War II led to another grouping—this time by full nationalization—that saw the arrival of British Railways in 1948. The company has been vilified over the years for many of its sweeping changes: the end of steam operations and the preference for diesel and electric traction; the so-called Beeching Axe that killed off many smaller lines—almost a third of the network—seen as being uneconomic at a time of growing private auto ownership. In the end, however, the size of government involvement led to privatization in the late 1990s. The rail infrastructure went to the national body Railtrack; freight operations sold off as six companies (although five were owned by the same buyer); and passenger operations sold as twenty-five franchises. The success of this operation is clouded by politics. Passenger numbers have increased but the split of operations and infrastructure is acknowledged by many as being a mistake.

The death of mainline steam in the 1960s led to a proliferation of preservation: a new railway mania that saw many classes of steam locomotive saved from the cutting torch and would lead to tourist lines, museums, and rail centers Perhaps the most triumphant example of this urge to preserve is the story of the Peppercorn "A1" class locomotive Tornado. The last of the class was scrapped in 1966 and none was saved for posterity. In 1990 the A1 Steam Locomotive Trust was formed with the dream of recreating an "A1." Remarkably, after nineteen years of effort, that locomotive, No. 60163 Tornado, moved under its own power in 2008.

Another "Black Five," this one is No. 45212, one of 18 preserved. It can be seen on the North Yorkshire Moors.

The holder of the world speed record for steam locomotives, Sir Nigel Gresley's beautiful "A4" Pacific design, No. 4468 Mallard a resident of the National railway Museum, York.

Another great designer, Oliver Bulleid of the Southern Railway designed the light Pacific "Battle of Britain" class. This is No. 34067 Tangmere.

Another "A4," this one No. 60007 named Sir Nigel Gresley after the class designer. It was originally numbered 4498.

"A4" Pacific No. 4464 Bittern, would be renumbered 60019. It is one of six to survive into preservation.

Bulleid Pacific "West Country" No. 34028 Eddystone runs regularly on the Swanage Railway in Southern England.

Stored in Ropley on the Watercress Line, "West Country" No 34016 Bodmin is named after the famous Cornish town and moor.

The "Schools" class was designed by Richard Maunsell of the Southern Railway. This is one of the forty in the class, No. 30926 Repton.

Great Britain

The British Rail "9F" class was one of the last steam designs to be built and No. 92220 Evening Star the last mainline steam loco to be built in the UK—until "A1" Tornado in 2008.

Built between 1936 and 1939, the "Dukedog" class of Great Western Railway 4-4-0s were withdrawn by 1960. The only one of the class preserved was No. 3217 Earl of Berkeley seen near Llangollen.

The "Battle of Britain" class Pacifics were named to honor the Royal Air Force. No. 34070 is named Manston after the famous RAF airbase in Kent.

Great Britain

BR Standard Class 2 2-6-0—four of the sixty-five-strong class survived into preservation.

Lancashire & Yorkshire Class 2F 0-6-0 No 957 designed by Barton-Wright and Class 3F No 1300 designed by Aspinall taken on the Keighley & Worth Valley Railway.

LMS, latterly British Railways, Mogul 2-6-0 No. 42968. The class was designed by Sir William Stanier and built 1933–34. The 42968 was the penultimate built and is the only one preserved, having been restored on the Severn Valley Railway.

Great Britain

"Merchant Navy" class Pacific No. 35005 Canadian Pacific is one of eleven of the class preserved and can be found on the Mid-Hants Railway.

The LNER "V2" class 2-6-2 were built 1936–44. Here is No. 60800 Green Arrow seen on the North Norfolk Railway. It is the only one of the 184 built to survive, although it isn't currently running having suffered a boiler failure.

The Great Western Railway 4900 or "Hall" class 4-6-0s were built between 1928 and 1943. Eleven of the 259 have been preserved, including No. 5972 Olton Hall that is used to pull the "Hogwarts Express" in the Harry Potter films.

Australasia

Puffing Billy runs on the mountain track it has always served, from Belgrave to Gembrook in the scenic Dandenong Ranges.

Australia

The history of railways in Australia begins in 1854 when the first line between Melbourne and Port Melbourne started operations. Thereafter, as everywhere in the Victorian world, the railway system of the various Australian colonies developed rapidly. Initially all track and rolling stock was imported, but by the 1880s most of the equipment was being made locally.

By Federation in 1901, all the states except Western Australia were linked by rail and more than 12,000 miles of track had been laid—but there had been no overall national view on this and the states used three different gauges: New South Wales adopted the European standard gauge of 1435 mm; Victoria and South Australia built with the broad Irish gauge of 1600 mm; and Tasmania, Queensland, Western Australia and parts of South Australia used the narrow 1067 mm gauge. This meant that a person wanting to travel from Perth to Brisbane on an east–west crossing of the continent had to change trains six times. While civilians could cope with this—and governments could ill afford to change it—wartime brought different requirements. World War II led to a war effort that required large quantities of goods and personnel to be moved quickly throughout Australia. While large strides towards standardization were made, it would not be until June 1995 that trains could travel between Brisbane and Perth, via Sydney, Melbourne and Adelaide on a standard gauge track. The three gauges still exist, but at least the state capitals are now linked by one uniform gauge.

As elsewhere, steam died out post-World War II and diesel-electric locomotives took over, with electric trains operating in dense suburban areas. Steam locomotives can still be found on scenic railways in New South Wales, Victoria and Tasmania.v

Thirlmere Railway Station in New South Wales Australia is the site of Australia's largest rail museum, the New South Wales Rail Transport Museum. This Type 2-6-0 Class G No. 2705.

Australasia

New Zealand

Railways reached New Zealand in 1862, when a horse-drawn private mining line opened at Dun Mountain near Nelson. New Zealand's first steam-powered public railway was a five-mile line from Christchurch to Ferrymead that opened in December 1863. Early railway building was slow. By 1870 New Zealand had just fifty miles of railway, all of it on the eastern and southern plains of the South Island, but in that year two important decisions were taken. First, Colonial Treasurer Julius Vogel announced a program to build more than a thousand miles of track that decade; and the government decided that all New Zealand railways would be built to the narrow 1,067mm gauge—even the tracks already built were converted—thus saving the country from the problems Australia had with mixed gauges.

By the end of the decade the government had been true to its word. Main lines between Christchurch and Invercargill and Christchurch and Dunedin had been completed by 1878. By 1880, New Zealand Railways had more than a thousand miles of track, and carried almost three million passengers and 830,000 tons of freight a year. The growth of the railways had the same effect as in Canada: it promoted central government and the old provincial governments were abolished in 1876.

The next major landmark in New Zealand railway history was the opening in 1908 of the North Island Main Trunk that connected Auckland and Wellington, cutting journey times to fourteen hours by 1924. This line took twenty-three years to build and opened up the whole of the North Island to development. By the early 1920s New Zealand Railways' figures had improved to more than six million tons of freight and an amazing twenty-eight million passengers a year by a population

The forty NZR "J" class steam locomotives were built by North British. No 21211 Gloria was converted to oil firing in 1996.

of around a million. World War II had a greater effect, 38.6 million journeys being recorded in 1943–44. At its height, in 1953, New Zealand boasted 3,500 miles of track.

The elephant in the room was that railway haulage of freight had been promoted by law. To protect railways against road competition restrictions on road haulage were introduced in 1936: freight could only be hauled a maximum of thirty miles. By 1977 this had been increased to a hundred miles, but in 1986 deregulation freed the road transport hauliers. Thirty percent of freight was hauled by rail in 1980: within a decade almost all of this had been lost to road. Within another five years privatization took place and New Zealand Rail Ltd became Tranz Rail Ltd. It was a massive failure and 2003 the government had to buy the railways back. Steam traction had disappeared from service in 1971 but preservation groups had done much to ensure New Zealand's steam heritage. While most early locomotives had been imported, mainly from Britain and the United States, New Zealand companies had built many of their own and many of these were preserved in the 1960s and 1970s. Best known of the preserved railways are the Bay of Islands Vintage Railway, Taieri Gorge Railway and Goldfields Steam Train Society. The North Island main line saw the return of steam in 2005.

The Weka Pass Railway line opened to Waikari in 1882 and was extended to Waiau by 1919. Regular passenger services were withdrawn in 1939 but opened again to preservation in the 1980s. One of the steam locomotives on the line is "A" class No. 428, built in New Zealand in 1909.

Rest of the World

The Rest of the World

While this book has concentrated on the major English-speaking nations, the rest of the world is no stranger to steam railway operations or preservation. Indeed, the major European nations—Germany, France, Italy—have a well-established preservation movement with major museums at such places as Milan (whose museum opened in 1968) and the two Museo Ferroviario Piemontese at Savigliano and Turin. Steam lasted longer in East Europe and many enthusiast tours recorded the last years of steam in countries such as Poland and

Over 400 steam locomotives are known to have been preserved in Brazil. The most famous museum operation in Brazil is the São João del Rei Preserved Railway, a narrow gauge line in central Brazil that has a number of preserved Baldwin 4-6-0s—here No. 42. The 1912-vintage Baldwins are preserved in the Museu Ferroviaria de São João del Rei.

Russia. After Europe lost its steam the enthusiast had to travel further afield to South Africa, India, and China where some steam trains still ply their trade.

Rest of the World

Graz-Köflacher-Eisenbahn (GKB) No. 671 can be found at the Technical Railway Museum in Lieboch, Styria, Austria. It is listed as the longest-serving steam locomotive of the world.

The Taurachbahn Steam Train runs from Mauterndorf to St. Andrä, one of many Austrian preserved steam lines. S12 (pictured here) was constructed in 1906 by Krauss Linz for the Salzkammergut Local Railway and pulled the last passenger train from Salzburg to St. Gilgen on September 30, 1957.

The "Sofazuegle" (sofa train) is a preserved train that travels between Nürtingen and Neuffen on the old Tälesbahn pulled by such locos as No. 11 of 1911.

Rest of the World

A typical modern German standard gauge industrial 0-6-0T.

One of the impressive and powerful meter-gauge 2-10-2Ts from the Harzquerbahn system, formerly part of the East German Railways (Deutsche Reichsbahn).

1930-built 760mm gauge 0-6-2T No 5 Gerlos of the Austrian Zillertalbahn, which runs from Jenbach to Mayrhofen.

Rest of the World

A German "Kriegslok" 2-10-0. One of thousands which were built for war service under the Third Reich, they subsequently served on many railway systems in Central and Eastern Europe until the 1970s and 1980s.

A Polish "Ol49" class 2-6-2 on a train of double-deck coaches. 112 of these were built for PKP (Polish Railways) in the early 1950s.

No. Ok22-31 is a Polish derivative of the classic Prussian "P8" class 4-6-0. Two examples have survived into preservation.

The Swiss Transportation Museum (Lucerne) contains examples of steam and electric locomotives and railroad cars from different parts of Switzerland over the last 150 years, displayed on more than a kilometer of track.

Rest of the World

This is 0-10-0 Er 797-86 in Kolomyia depot in the Ukraine. One of nearly 3,000 built, it regularly runs mainline steam excursions.

With nearly 100,000 miles of track the Russian rail system was one of the world's biggest until it was broken up following the collapse of the Soviet Union. As with all railways, much of the donkey work in yards and sheds was done by small shunting locomotives—sometimes called "Pony engines." This is a fine looking 9P series Russian 0-6-0 loco.

A miniature replica of a classic American nineteenth century 4-4-0.

The first railway line in Iberia was built in 1848 between Barcelona and Mataró in Catalonia. This is a replica of the Mataro engine that was produced in 1948 to mark Spanish Railways' hundredth anniversary.

The meter-gauge Engerth, formerly No. 12 of the – Villablino railway in Northern Spain, where it operated until the 1980s, and seen here preserved at the Basque Railway Museum.

Developed by Herbert William Garratt, a British locomotive engineer, these articulated steam locomotives performed powerfully in South Africa with the "GL" delivered in 1930 being the most powerful. East African Railways, "59" class 4-8-2+2-8-4s saw service until the 1980s—a favorite of many a steam enthusiast.

The LNER's "A4" class No. 60009 was named after the then newly-formed Union of South Africa and a springbok plaque was added on the side of the locomotive April 12, 1954. On October 24, 1964, it hauled the last booked steam-hauled train from Kings Cross but went into preservation and sees regular use on mainline steam excursions.

South African 4-8-2 "19D" class No. 3321. The Class 19 was designed by Col. F.R. Collins and delivered by Berliner Machinenbau. The 19D, built by Krupp, Borsig and Skoda before the war, was continued by North British Locomotive Co. which built the last fifty.

South African Railways 25NC Class 4-8-4 No. 3405 was built by North British in Glasgow and can be seen as a static exhibit at the Buckinghamshire Railway Center. She worked such prestige services as the "Blue Train" until the late 1970s and dieselization. Thanks to the generosity of the Transnet Museum Preservation Control Board she was returned to the UK, arriving in October 1991

Another "19D," No. 3323.

Romania once had an extensive system of narrow-gauge railways—particularly forestry liness—and runs a number of standard gauge mainline specials. The Resita Locomotive Museum shown here has a number of static exhibits.

There are some 250 steam locomotives preserved in Turkey including TCDD No. 45051 at Bandirma train station.

Japanese National Railways stopped steam operations in December 1975, but Hokkaido now has a tradition of running single and double headed C11 2-6-4T engines in almost guaranteed snow from Kushiro in the winter.

The Ambarawa Railway Museum in In donesia has a collection of twenty-one steam locomotives including four that are operational. C2001 was constructed by Hartmann and was originally Nederlands Indische Spoorweg Mij 351. The 0-6-2T was one of a number of similar "skirt" tanks, all of which worked branches based on Gundeh and around Solo into the 1970s.

Rest of the World

Datong in Shanxi province, China, is a major coal-mining town with a substantial railway locomotive works that attracted increasing numbers of railway enthusiasts from the 1970s as steam operations died out in Europe. This is Gongjian 1019, a static exhibit at Datong Museum.

Manzhouli lies in the verdant grasslands of Mongolia and is the border location where the Trans-Manchurian arm of the Trans-Siberian Railway heads toward Beijing. It is a significant coalmining town and had a big locomotive depot that steam enthusiasts discovered in the 1970s. It also boasts the Square of Steam Locomotive in which, it is said, sits a special locomotive always used by Chairman Mao.

China Railways SY 0309 "Mikado" 2-8-2 was built at Tangshan, in China. It now resides in Beijing's 751 Art District, Dashanz renumbered.

Rest of the World

Today India has less steam than hitherto. Apart from occasional special trains, there are just two mountain railways and a couple of small industrial operations—very different to even five years ago. Here, two steam engines refill with water at Agra station.

The National Rail Museum in New Delhi opened on February 1, 1977. With eleven acres of land and over a hundred exhibits it has in its collection the 1855 2-2-2 Fairy Queen and many other locomotives including this one from the Jaipur State Railway. It stands at the head of Palace on Wheels coaches, saloons from the former princely states of Rajasthan.

Another NRM exhibit, Darjeeling Himalayan Railway "B" class No. Until recently the DHR was another mecca for steam enthusiasts.